RAILWAY RAMBLES AROUND DONCASTER

C. T. GOODE

1987

ISBN 1 870313 02 X

72 Woodland Drive, Anlaby. Hull. HU10 7HX

RAILWAY RAMBLES AROUND DONCASTER

'Not another picture book on Doncaster railways!' I can hear people saying. Apart from a few photographs which are worth a second airing and are perhaps too significant to omit, I think that most of the material collected is unpublished and some of it unusual. It is interesting, too, that I and my contemporaries tended to take photographs more of the ex Great Central line subjects than of trains at Great Northern locations, probably because these subjects were too commonplace at the time, though there were excellent places such as Arksey and Rossington to visit, all very photogenic.

Doncaster was indeed an excellent place to study motive power of all kinds, and if one waited long enough, then it was likely that every type of engine would eventually come past. During the war I did actually see a Southern engine at one time on an ambulance train, though nothing steamed in from the GWR. With the Race traffic in September each year traffic was bustling enough, but it was the awakening of the coalfield which brought the interesting and often eccentric railways to the area. The L & Y Dearne Valley branch was 'cute' and different, while the products of the Hull & Barnsley were memorable without being too pompous and smacked more of country branch lines than purposeful coal-movers. Probably the nearest thing to Paradise was a trip along the Denaby branch on a hot summer's afternoon. Now, except for the main routes to the four points of the compass, some disfigured by knitting, all the evocative peripherals have gone, even big, bustling Bullcroft Junction which had actually ceased bustling long before 1939, but looked every inch the part.

C. Tony Goode BA.
Anlaby, Hull. 1987

4

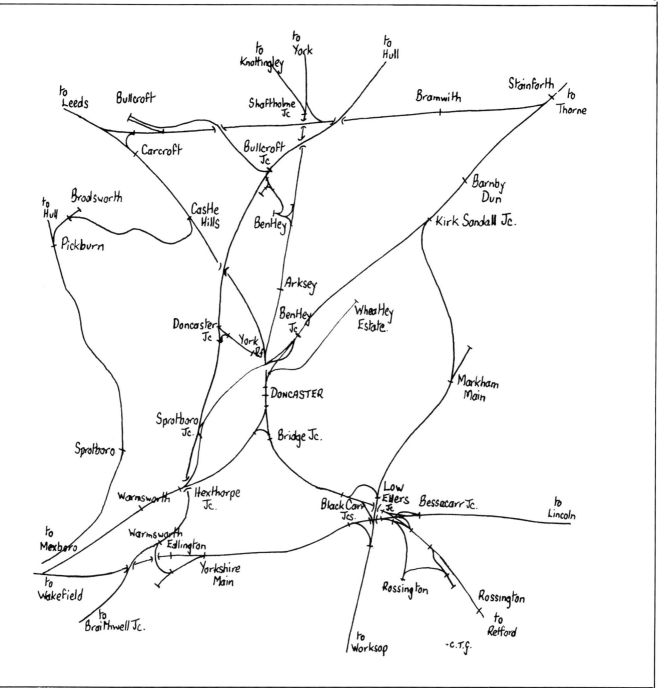

BRITISH RAILWAYS

C 554 X

DONCASTER RACES

FIRST RACE 2.0 p.m.   LAST RACE 4.30 p.m. EACH DATE

EXCURSIONS TO

DONCASTER

SATURDAY MAY 23rd
WHIT MONDAY and TUESDAY
MAY 25th and 26th

OUTWARD JOURNEY

		am	M.O. am	S.O. pm	Tu.O. pm	M.O. pm	S.O. pm	Return fares third class s d
Sheffield (Victoria)	dep.	10 0	11 48	12 7	12 7	12 30	12 36	*3/3
Broughton Lane	,,	—	—	—	—	12 36	12 42	*2/11
Rotherham (Central)	,,	10 13	—	12 20	12 20	12 45	12 51	*2/5
Kilnhurst (Central)	,,	10S 21	—	—	—	12 53	12 58	*2/0
Mexborough	,,	10 28	—	12 33	12 33	1 0	1 6	*1/4
Conisbrough	,,	10 32	pm	—	—	—	1 10	*/11
Doncaster	arr.	10 42	12 23	12 48	12 46	1 12	1 20	

RETURN JOURNEY

		A pm	pm	S.O. pm	pm	Tu.O. pm	M.O. pm	M.O. pm
Doncaster	dep.	4 43	5 39	5 45	6 24	6 32	6 35	7 7
Conisbrough	arr.	4 53	—	—	6 33	—	—	—
Mexborough	,,	5 5	5 51	5 59	6 39	6 45	—	7 20
Kilnhurst (Central)	,,	5 12	—	—	6 45	—	—	7 29
Rotherham (Central)	,,	5 21	6 6	6 15	6 55	7 0	—	7 37
Broughton Lane	,,	5 29	—	—	—	—	—	7 48
Sheffield (Victoria)	,,	5 37	6 23	6 30	7 9	7 15	7 15	7 55

A—Runs 15 minutes later on Saturday.   Tu.O.—Tuesday only.
S and S.O.—Saturday only.   M.O.—Monday only.

*—Day Return fares. Passengers holding such tickets are permitted to travel outward and return by any train on day of issue

If the races are cancelled and notice is given to this Region in time to cancel these facilities the fares paid by intending passengers will be refunded on application

Tickets can be obtained IN ADVANCE at stations and agencies

Further information will be supplied on application to stations, offices, agencies, or to K. A. Kindon, District Passenger Superintendent, Sheffield (Victoria) Station, (Tel: 25167, Ext. 6) or C. Dandridge, Commercial Superintendent, Liverpool Street Station, London, E.C.2. (Tel: BIshopsgate 7600).

CONDITIONS OF ISSUE

These tickets are issued subject to the conditions of issue of ordinary tickets where applicable and also to the special conditions as set out in the Bye-Laws, Regulations and Conditions in the published notices

LUGGAGE ALLOWANCES are as set out in these general notices

Children under three years of age, free; three years and under fourteen, half-fares

April, 1953.

Published by The Railway Executive (Eastern Region).   Printed in Great Britain.   W. A. SMITH (Leeds) LTD.

1. The former South Yorkshire Railway from Barnsley and Mexborough to Doncaster and beyond to Thorne and along the south bank of the Humber was busy with all kinds of traffic, and the two miles or so out of Doncaster westwards to Hexthorpe Jc. were in time quadrupled with access to the extensive Great Northern goods yards on Doncaster Carrs.

Here B16 4-6-0 No.61457 passes Hexthorpe Flatts with a heavy mixed freight.

2. A similar mixed freight is seen here, hauled by K3 2-6-0 No.61829. Both workings would have been made up on the GN section.

3. In the 1950s it was decided to revive the old pre 1939 LMS workings between Sheffield Midland station and Hull, this time working the train out and home from Hull (Botanic Gardens). This particular working left Doncaster at 10.24am., ahead of the 10.32am. Hull-Liverpool Cen., and is seen here headed by D49 No.62754 'The Berkeley'. The route taken after Mexborough was up and round on to the Midland at Swinton.

4. There was well organised turmoil when Doncaster Race Week came in September, with several days of excursion train activity, chiefly from Barnsley and Sheffield to a special station at St. James' Bridge, just south of the main Central station and at the end of the abovementioned quadrupled lines. All kinds of motive power was pressed into service, as here where J39 0-6-0 No.64725 is about to run off the goods lines at Hexthorpe Jc. with a returning race special.

5. St. James' Bridge station with J11s Nos.64403 and 64442 sporting express headcodes ready to leave. With use on only one week in the year the station with its large canopy must have been an extravagance.

6. Each weekday Pilkingtons glassworks at Kirk Sandall sent a train of its products to Mexborough and the yards, usually via Doncaster station and Hexthorpe Jc. (as here), though sometimes via the avoiding line. The train was always headed by the Barnby Dun pilot, a J6 0-6-0.

7. A B1 passes Warmsworth Lime Sidings with the Hull-Liverpool Cen. train. The little box was in an excellent location, part time with ten levers and the steps on the right of the picture afforded an airy panorama.

8. Conisbrough was the intermediate station before Mexborough and had a fine building in the house style of the Manchester, Sheffieild & Lincolnshire, later Great Central company with its decorative barge-boarding. Now, alas, all but the farthest section in the photograph has been pulled down and the site is unstaffed.

9. Beyond Conisbrough at Lowfield Jc. was the point where the Hull & Barnsley's Denaby branch came in from the colliery and from Wrangbrook Jc. way to the north through beautiful countryside (see No.57). Here a diesel hauled excursion train comes off the branch and heads for Mexborough.

10. A little further on was Denaby Crossing, a skew affair where the busy road passed between Denaby Main and Mexborough. Here one of the cheeky little green and cream trolleybuses of the Mexborough & Swinton Traction Company, No.23 waits patiently to cross. Note the long trolley poles and the safety net above the wire support standards. All the structures in this photograph have now gone.

11. A poorish but active view taken from the footbridge at Denaby crossing looking towards Denaby Main. The colliery gunpowder sidings are down to the right, while the row of cottages has vanished completely.

12. A general view of the crossing, showing the tall signal box and giving some idea of the skew. Mexborough station has now all but vanished.

13. Included here is a picture of No.2395 (later 69999), the huge Beyer-Garratt locomotive used to perform the banking duties on Wentworth bank near Barnsley and shedded at Mexborough, where there was quite a large depot. The engine spent quite a time under repair at Doncaster, due to leaky pipes.

14. Back to Hexthorpe Jc. and looking towards Doncaster with a shortish and neat train of sand passing by. On the left is the avoiding line which, as its name implies, avoids Doncaster and runs from a point at Bentley Jc. on the SYR line to Thorne.

15. A B1 No.61165 heads a Cleethorpes-Sheffield holiday train homewards off the avoiding line.

16. Trains in trouble could gain assistance from the banking engine at Sprotborough Jc., situated at the foot of the incline up to Hexthorpe Jc. For this purpose an often superannuated old GC locomotive from Mexborough shed would be kept here by day, the crew whiling away the hours in the signal box with tea and cards. Doncaster shed did at times provide a J3 or J6 for the duty, and on one occasion the prototype L1 No.9000 in green livery did a day's stint. In the picture B5 4-6-0 No.1689 puts in the hours. The line nearest to the camera is the H & B and GC Joint line, of which more later. The other line is the avoiding line looking towards Bentley Jc., while the diagonal line across the view is a signal guy rope!

17. On at least one occasion a J11 0-6-0 acted as banker, seen here with Richard Brown on the unusual side of Sprotborough Jc. signal box.

18. A good shot of the cabin taken from the avoiding line, on which it actually turned its back, since all the operating windows faced the other side.

19. First station out to the north east of Doncaster was Barnby Dun. never a very busy spot and with two platform faces for the Thorne direction and only one for the other way on the four track layout. Here a train of tractors passes through on the slow line.

20. Stainforth & Hatfield station seen on a winter's day looking towards Doncaster. The layout has been heavily remodelled here, where the West Riding & Grimsby line to Carcroft and Leeds branches off.

21. The Up 'Yorkshire Pullman' comes off the Hull branch on to the GC line for Doncaster at Thorne Jc., headed by V3 2-6-2T No.67635.

22. Activity between Stainforth and Barnby Dun as a WD 2-8-0 No.90287 brings a train of empties towards Doncaster.

23. In the opposite direction a Midland Region Beyer Garratt, probably from Hasland Sidings takes a train to Frodingham (Scunthorpe).

24. Immediately to the north of Doncaster on the main line to York was Arksey station, from where B1 No.61120 is seen leaving with a Down slow working, shortly before closure in August 1951.

25. In the other direction to the south lay Rossington, seen here with a full turnout of staff and permanent way men. The difference in the platform levels is noteworthy.

26. The next station south was Bawtry, seen here looking north and with an extremely tall Up home signal just visible in the distance. All the last three stations mentioned had buildings of similar design.

27. The old frontage of Doncaster station, long before No.1 platform was put in and things were modernised. The noticeboard offered a comprehensive range of tempting destinations.

28. First stop out on the line to Leeds was Carcroft & Adwick-le-Street, one of two stations (the other was South Elmsall) built in a sort of Dutch cum Bavarian style.

29. Really, the first untimetabled stop out on the Leeds line was a miners' halt situated at Bentley Crossing.

30. A close-up of the structure at South Elmsall.

31. Looking north from North Bridge, the layout of Marshgate jc. at Doncaster can be seen in 1951, with the Leeds lines off to the left, York straight ahead and Thorne to the right. The colour lights are in position but not yet in use. The avoiding line crosses in the background.

32. Deltic D9003 crosses the canal bridge at Marshgate Jc. twenty years later with an Edinburgh-King's Cross express.

33. In the other direction seen from North Bridge Deltic 55-013 comes through with the Down 'Flying Scotsman'. Note the old station buildings seen prominently back left.

34. Seen from platform 8 on Doncaster station on 23rd July, 1971 are three Class 31s with No.5622 on empty stock and Nos.5559 and 5845 on a train of hoppers.

35. The north end of Doncaster station is seen from the commanding view offered by a multi-storey car park as 'Western' No.1023 comes through on a special working on 20th November, 1976.

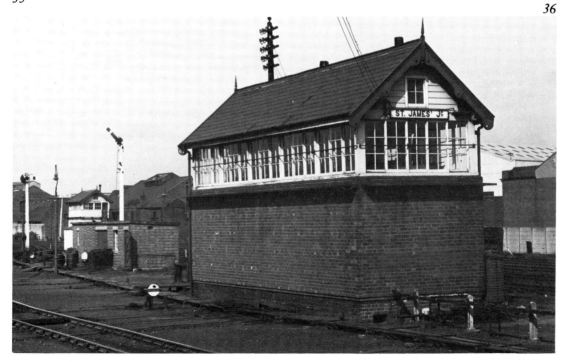

36. St. James' Jc. signal box at the south end of Doncaster station layout, with the GC Cherry Tree cabin in the background which controlled the passenger lines to Hexthorpe Jc.

37. Looking across the GC lines, on which is B1 No.1168, to St. James' Bridge station and beyond to see the GN main line running away under Balby bridge in the background.

38. Doncaster motive power depot with N2 No.69535, B1 No.61231 and one other.

39. LNER, ex GN 'Atlantic' No.4400 'on shed'.

40. No.1402, the GN 'Royal Engine', gets away south with the Royal Train in July 1911.

41. A pristine B1 waits at Doncaster station with a mixture of old and new signalling, looking north.

42. D49 'Hunt' and 'Shire' class (nearest camera) in deplorable condition back on to the mid morning slow train to York.

43. A local diesel unit from Sheffield passes St. James' bridge station on the left and a multiple pile-up of vehicles on the right.

44. Bridge Jc. on the main line at the south end of Doncaster in 1952 when the mechanical signalling was fading away. The sixteen arm signalling gantry is visible.

45. The old turntable from the north end of Doncaster station which was relocated at the loco. depot. Sand Bank signal box is seen in the background.

46. Frenchgate Jc. signal box just north of the station under North Bridge, once a busy spot when the A1 road crossed here on the level before the bridge was built.

47. There was a convenient link line across the north side of the Doncaster area between Carcroft in the west and Stainforth to the east, handy for Leeds-Cleethorpes traffic avoiding Doncaster. Set on this was a station at Kirk Bramwith, which seems to have been used for goods purposes only. The signal box survived for many years after the rest had gone.

48. On this line was situated the little known swing bridge across the Don, controlled by a rather primitive pair of GN stop signals, the nearer of which seems too close to the hazard to give much safety margin. Note the distant signal placed on the correct side of the bridge so as to make wiring easier.

49. The GN main line ceased at Shaftholme Jc., north of Doncaster and the line to Newcastle ran on as the North Eastern Railway. At this point the Lancashire & Yorkshire ran in from Knottingley and, in fact, Scottish trains ran this way before the NER line via York was completed. The first station from Shaftholme along the L & Y was Askern with its four-square building and notice 'for the use of the Parish Council only'.

50. Womersley was much more imposing and still survives at the time of writing. The Stanhope family lived at nearby Womersley Hall.

51. The Midland and the North Eastern put in a useful jointly operated line running north-south between Swinton and Knottingley, forming an excellent through route for important traffic, especially during wartime. The stations all tended to look alike, comprising a central oblong house with two flanking single storied gables. The nearest to Doncaster was Moorthorpe where quite a volume of excursion traffic was dealt with on holiday Saturdays.

52. (also above).

53. Frickley, to the south, now closed, was more rural and seems to have owed its existence to the hall nearby.

54. In 1885 the Hull & Barnsley opened its line from the South Yorkshire coalfield to the north of Doncaster, running eastwards from the Cudworth area through Upton and Kirk Smeaton, where stations were optimistically sited. Kirk Smeaton, seen here, was one of the prettiest settings in the Doncaster area.

55. 8F 2-8-0 No.48167 passes Upton with a westbound coal train.

56. West of Kirk Smeaton was Upton & North Elmsall.

57. Between the two stations lay Wrangbrook Jc., the point where two branches went south, one to Denaby and later to Lowfield Jc. and the GC (see No.9), and to Wath. The camera here looks east towards Hull with the branches leading away to the right.

58. Here an engine and brake vans come off the Denaby branch at Wrangbrook. The yard beyond is on the Wath branch.

59. First stop southwards on the Denaby branch was Pickburn & Brodsworth, a station in a modest way in the early days but latterly a point of entry to Brodsworth colliery. Here a WD 2-8-0 and brake vans wait to enter the colliery branch.

60. The first passenger train for years passes Pickburn signal box as B1 No.61166 comes through on an RCTS special from Denaby.

61

62

61. 62. Two views of Sprotborough station, a wooden structure almost identical to Pickburn except for the chimneys, with the minimum facilities.

63. The tunnel mouth at Cadeby, looking north towards Sprotborough.

64 & 65. At the beginning of this century a further branch was put down to serve collieries at Frickley, Hickleton and Wath, and a modest passenger service ran between little stations and out to Kirk Smeaton on the main line. First station south was Moorhouse & South Elmsall.

65. The smart brick building and copious gents' are seen to advantage here.

66. Then came Hickleton & Thurnscoe, of similar style, though with a wooden platform. Wath terminus had a similar building which still exists at the time of writing.

67. The smart little signal box at Hickleton station. The Colliery cabin was similar, a little further down the line.

68. The last train leaves Moorhouse on 6th April, 1929.

69. At about the same time the Lancashire & Yorkshire decided to send a long branch line, known as the Dearne Valley, out from the Wakefield and Crofton area into the Doncaster district to glean coal, running eastwards to complicated connections with the GN and GE companies south east of the town on the Carrs. Thus, in L & Y and LMS days one had the luxury of really 'foreign' engines working out of their home territory. Here a WD 2-8-0 brings a train eastwards from Cadeby colliery.

70. Another few yards would take it over the substantial viaduct at Conisbrough across the Don.

71. Equally substantial was the great girder viaduct taking the Dearne Valley line over the GN main line.

72. The first passenger working at Edlington Halt on the opening day.

72a. On the last day of operation the push and pull train, with No.41284 in charge, gets a changeover of tail and headlamp at Edlington Halt, where the oil lamp standards on the platform survived to the last. To the left is a Motive Power Inspector, while the driver collects his share of fans wanting autographs in the background.

73. Twenty years on and a local working out of Doncaster Decoy yard waits at Yorkshire Main Siding cabin.

74. A consortium of companies, GC.,GN.,L&Y.,MR., and NE built a line down from the GC line to Thorne to the north east of Doncaster, over the GN and the end of the Dearne Valley line just mentioned into virtually new mining territory, ending up again on the GC near Worksop. On the line of route were collieries at Harworth, Maltby and Dinnington, while the section north of the GN was really access only for trains to and from the NE system, though there was one colliery at Armthorpe which WD 2-8-0 No.90685 passes with empties.

75. Further south 8F 2-8-0 No.48638 is seen with a lightweight train.

76. Approaching Tickhill & Wadworth station is WD 2-8-0 No.90078 with a train of empties.

77. From the outset of operations in September 1908 a token passenger service ran between Doncaster and Worksop, the motive power and stock usually supplied by the GC system. Here a 4-4-2 tank poses with the first train at Tickhill station.

78. There were other similar stations at Maltby, seen here, and Dinnington. None was near the places it served, though Anston at the south end was fairly well positioned.

79. The signals and cabins were of the best GC pattern, and Maltby colliery yard was well covered with cabins at the north and south ends.

80.81. The Hull & Barnsley was obviously not content with its access to the South Yorkshire coalfield over its main line, and branches from Wrangbrook, so joined forces with the GC to provide a line southwards from Aire Jc. (Carlton) on its main line towards Doncaster where there was a station at York Road on a terminal spur, followed by a connection to the GC avoiding line further south before the new route disappeared beyond Edlington and eventually reached the Dinnington area. The line was distinctly H & B in style from the north to Bullcroft Jc. and to a point north of York Road, but thoroughly GC south of this. Nothing much happened on the line, the most activity being between Warmsworth, which was the connection for Yorkshire Main Colliery, and via Sprotborough Jc. to Doncaster and its hungry locomotives.

Here the line is shown under construction at the place where it crossed beneath the avoiding line at Hexthorpe Jc. The girders will be dropped into position below.

82. Most attractive was the little cabin at Low Ellers Jc. at the point where trains could run round a spur down to the Up side of the GN main line, seen here with its loo and horseshoe. The loop line is visible in front, the main line out of sight behind.

83. A contractor's train between Doncaster Jc. and Sprotborough Jc.

84. Weird, perhaps, but on the H & B portion of line near Pollington a lifting bridge had to be provided over the river Aire. This was done as a token gesture, since no high masted vessels ever passed and no lifting gear or motors were ever provided.

85. Bullcroft Jc. was one of the most active places on the H & B and GC Joint line, with the largest signal box and two reasonable sized yards. These housed traffic for the collieries at Bentley and Bullcroft, the latter at Skellow reached by a long single line branch. Here the twain meet as an H & B domeless tank engine encounters a GC locomotive in the sidings. The wagons visible are marked 'Bullcroft' and 'Camroux'.

86. A view from the Great North Road bridge of Doncaster Jc., incidentally the only signal box in the area to carry the name of the town. The line curves left to Bullcroft Jc. and eventually Hull, while to the right is the trackbed of one of the spurs to York Road terminus.

87. Temporary engine shed at the terminus, with a contractor's engine outside, probably the same one as depicted in No.83.

88. A rare view of Warmsworth Jc. taken in 1934. The lines on the left lead to Yorkshire Main colliery. To the left to where the engine is waiting is the site of a platform intended as part of a passenger service over the whole line, which never materialised.

89. A Thompson rebuild of a GC 2-8-0 No.63828 comes off the Joint line from Doncaster Jc. towards Sprotborough Jc. with a train of empties. Adjacent is Fowler's Tank factory siding.

90. On the line from Doncaster to Lincoln, which left the GN at Black Carr Jc. and which was shared by that company with the Great Eastern. Here was Haxey Junction, a remote place and with rather gaunt premises not unlike the original buildings at Doncaster Central.

91. The Sheffield (Midland) to Hull working sets out on its homeward run in July 1951. See No.3.

G 590

THE **TATTOO** ALDERSHOT
HALF-DAY RESTAURANT CAR EXCURSION
(DEAN & DAWSON'S)
TO
ALDERSHOT
THURSDAY 8th JUNE 1939

OUTWARD JOURNEY			RETURN FARES THIRD CLASS	RETURN JOURNEY		
		p.m.	s. d.			a.m. 9th
Cleethorpes	dep.	12 7	11 0	ALDERSHOT	dep.	1 33
Grimsby Docks	„	12 17	11 0	(Government Sidings)		
Grimsby Town	„	12 25	11 0	Peterborough (North)	arr.	5 20
Scunthorpe & Frodingham	„	1 5	11 0	Grantham	„	6 5
Doncaster (Central)	„	1 55	11 0	*Lincoln (L·N·E·R)	„	8 0
Retford	„	2 17	10 0	*Sleaford	„	6 57
Newark	„	2 45	9 0	*Boston	„	7 32
		noon		*Skegness	„	9 4
*Mablethorpe	„	12 0	10 0	*Sutton-on-Sea	„	9 8
		p.m.		*Mablethorpe	„	9 14
*Sutton-on-Sea	„	12 7	10 0	Newark	„	6 24
*Skegness	„	12 4	9 6	Retford	„	6 49
*Boston	„	1 6	8 3	Doncaster (Central)	„	7 12
*Sleaford	„	1 46	9 0	Scunthorpe & Frodingham	„	7 55
*Lincoln (L·N·E·R)	„	1 56	9 6	Grimsby Town	„	8 40
Grantham	„	3 5	8 3	Grimsby Docks	„	8 45
Peterborough (North)	„	3 50	6 9	Cleethorpes	„	8 55
ALDERSHOT	arr.	7 58				
(Government Sidings)						

* Passengers from these Stations change at Grantham in each direction and go forward at 3-5 p.m.

In the event of the Tattoo being either postponed or cancelled this train will not run provided the Company receives notice at the Station of departure in sufficient time to cancel the arrangements
Rail Tickets and bills can be obtained in advance at the Stations and Agencies

ENCLOSURE "D" TICKETS
Admission Tickets for "D" Enclosure only can be obtained at 1/6 each (no reduction for children) at the stations when Rail Tickets are purchased
These tickets are for Open Air Enclosure Seats, not numbered and reserved (Ticket guarantees seat) see Tattoo announcements
Early application should be made as there are only a limited number available

TATTOO ADMISSION TICKETS can be obtained on application by post direct from the Secretary, The Tattoo, Steele's Road, Stanhope Lines, Aldershot. It is important that visitors to the Tattoo should obtain their admission tickets in advance and early application is essential

The Aldershot and District Traction Co., Ltd., will arrange a service of omnibuses between Aldershot Station and the Tattoo Ground. Single fare 4d.

RESTAURANT CAR
TEA 1/1   **SUPPER 2/9**
(Including Gratuities)
Tickets obtainable in advance at the Stations.   Number limited

For further information apply to the District Manager, Lincoln or Peterborough; or the Passenger Manager, Liverpool Street Station, London, E.C.2

CONDITIONS OF ISSUE
Day, Half-day and Evening tickets are issued subject to the conditions applicable to tickets of these descriptions as shown in the Company's Time Tables.   For LUGGAGE ALLOWANCES also see Time Tables

London, May 1939

X Via Canonbury and Acton Wells X

L·N·E·R

All the photographs were taken by the Author, or are from his collection except in the following cases:-

W. Ashton	*– 29,40,88*
P. Cookson	*– 21,53,55,58*
T. G. Flinders	*– 12,14,18,32,33,34,35,36,47,50,71,82,90*
Heyday Publishing Co.	*– 25,26,27,49,66*
M. Mitchell	*– 69*
M. Nicholson	*– 67*
Sheffield City Library	*– 72*
N.E. Stead	*-5*

Other books by the Author include the following:—

'The Dearne Valley Railway'

'Railway Rambles on the Hull & Barnsley Railway'

'Railways of East Yorkshire'   (Oakwood Press)

'Railway Rambles on the Cheshire Lines'

'The Railways of Leeds & Bradford'

Designed and Printed by Swannack, Brown & Co. Ltd., 13a Anlaby Road, Hull.